She's at YOUR DOOR

EXPOSING THE ESCORT INDUSTRY

VINCE GOLIA

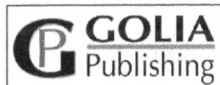

GP GOLIA
Publishing

WELLINGTON, FL

Golia Publishing
Wellington, FL

ISBN: 978-0-6156657-3-3

Cover photo: Vince Golia
Cover model: Rachel Fry
Cover and interior design: Gary A. Rosenberg

Printed in the United States of America.

Contents

This book is dedicated to the highest paid "professional women" in America. May they depart the escort profession with their financial objectives achieved and their souls unblemished.

> *"When I am good, I am very good.*
> *When I am bad, I am even better."*
> —MAE WEST,
> AMERICAN ACTRESS AND SEX SYMBOL

Acknowledgments

My thanks to my wonderful children, who inspire me each day with their love and support. I am grateful to my son, who spent countless hours examining and correcting his father's grammatically incorrect sentences. I want to also acknowledge my daughter for her spontaneous, humorous, and perspicacious comments regarding the nature of the subject matter. I am especially indebted to Michele Matrisciani (www.bookchic.net) for taking the time to read my book and share her extensive knowledge of the publication process.

Reader's Note

The information in this book comes from my own personal experience. This book takes you through the process from when the client dials an escort service to what transpires afterward. Each escort agency is unique, so another individual's experiences may differ from my own. The names of the escorts and the agencies have been withheld, to protect the not so innocent. To make your reading experience more pleasurable, I have designated a guide to the acronyms and terms used throughout the book. Please take a moment to familiarize yourself with these terms before starting Chapter One.

Preface

I am an escort driver in South Florida; I have worked for six different agencies. While composing this book, I drove escorts for two exceedingly distinctive agencies. I have never owned an escort agency but have been a dispatcher and a manager in the owner's absence. I have worn many hats in South Florida since I moved from New York to Delray Beach, Florida, in 1990. I have been an entrepreneur, owning a hair salon in Boca Raton. I have worked for corporate America (best pay, worst experience), and I have been an honest salesman many times over. I spent two years doing commercials and taking extra roles in movies. I have even taught theology in a Catholic high school in Fort Lauderdale for three years. I am an amateur entomologist and have two insects named after me. If you Google my name and add the word "insects," you will find more than a dozen different articles connected to my discoveries. I have also coauthored two papers pertaining to exotic insects I discovered in Florida.

In social situations, the question I am asked most often is, "How did you get into the escort industry?" I started working in the escort business seven years ago. While glancing through the classified section of a local newspaper, I came across an interesting category known as "Adult Entertainment." There was an employment ad for women who wanted to make a substantial income, as well as drivers. With apprehension, I called and was asked my age, the year and make of my car, and my available hours. After setting up an interview, I was told to bring my driver's license and a utility bill matching the address on the license. I suspect this was a way of eliminating any undercover officers from applying. I'm not sure how effective it is, but it's common practice with most agencies. The initial interview took place in a restaurant in Boca Raton, Florida, and was conducted by a middle-aged woman. I was never called back, but my persistence paid off when I was hired a month later.

Guide to Acronyms
& Terminology

Asian BJ—when a woman suckles the tip of your penis, as if she is drinking out of a nipple tip bottle. (Pleasurable, even if she is not from the other side of the world.)

ATF—acronym for all time favorite. Common term found in escort reviews.

Barred Out—client or escort has difficulty speaking or walking due to effect of too much Xanax (alprazolam). Xanax is also referred to as "bars" or "sticks."

Bait and Switch—when a client expects the girl he selected from the magazine or Internet to show up at his door and quickly realizes he has been deceived.

BBBJ (bareback blow job)—old school term for an escort who is willing to perform oral sex without a condom, provided she likes what she sees. (Actually, a thorough examination with the proper lighting is highly recommended for both parties. The term has been replaced with GFE.)

Blues or Roxies—a generic pill that contains 30 mg of Oxycodone. Roxicodone is the number one reason there are countless pain clinics throughout South Florida. (They are immensely popular with escorts and strippers.)

Booting—also known as shooting, banging, blasting. Using a needle to mainline drugs into your bloodstream. (The main reason it takes so long for the escorts to come out of the public restrooms and client's bathrooms.)

Call—a reference to the actual booking by the dispatcher. The escort may be going to a call but may not book the call if she doesn't collect the fee.

Cancellation Fee—fee paid to an escort and/or driver when she is rejected.

Cash 'n' Dash—when an escort takes the client's money up front and gives the client an excuse to leave the premises with no intention of returning. (Not when I am driving.)

CBJ—acronym for covered blow job. (Safe, but not pleasurable for either party.)

Checking In—when a girl collects the money from the client and calls the driver and/or the agency with the profitable news.

Checking Out—when the girl calls the driver and/or the agency to let them know the call is over. (The driver had better be less than two minutes away.)

CIM—acronym for cum in mouth. (Escort can spit or swallow at her discretion.)

Clock Watchers—also known as a pain in the ass. A client who is usually high and who continually keeps track of the allotted escort hour. Escorts who are excessive clock-watchers are considered unprofessional.

Coke Hold—may be an escort's favorite position. When a client, who is usually under the influence of cocaine, continuously converses with the escort. When the hour is up, the escort will either extend or leave without performing any sexual acts.

DATO—acronym for dining at the orifice, also known as tossing the salad or a rim job. The escort will allow client to perform analingus, a form of oral sex on her asshole. (An acquired taste I may never develop.)

DATY—acronym for dining at the Y. The escort allows client to perform cunnilingus, a form of oral sex on her vagina. (At least have her shower first.)

DFK—acronym for deep French kissing. (I hope she used mouthwash after her last date).

DP—acronym for double penetration. The term usually applies to one penis in the vagina and one penis in the anus. However, two penises in any orifice may suffice.

Drop—the driver drops the agency's money to the office or to another driver.

Drug Whore/Garbage Can—a reference to a drug user who will use any drug that is available at the time.

Extending—the escort has collected the money for at least another hour. (Everyone is elated).

FS—acronym for full service. This includes oral sex and/ or intercourse. (Despite the term "full," it never includes anal sex.)

Geeker—a client who is very high on crack cocaine, exceedingly impatient, and incessantly in motion.

GFE—acronym for girlfriend experience. The client has expectations of kissing the escort on the lips. (Are you kidding me, do you know where those lips have been all night? The john may also expect a BBBJ.)

Golden Shower—client would like escort to urinate on him. Usually, she will get an extra fee for humiliating him. (My guess is the service will be performed in the shower or bathtub.)

Hard—a term regarding the use or purchase of crack cocaine (not a reference to the client's penis).

Hobbyist—also known as whoremaster or whoremonger. A client who routinely calls for escorts. (Quite possibly a sex addict.)

Hooker—a popular term which may have been coined from an area in New York frequented by street-walkers known as Corlear's Hook. Legend has it General Joseph Hooker of the Union Army had a following of prostitutes known as "Hookers Brigade."

Hot Plate—escort is paid plenty of cash to wrap a piece of plastic on client's chest prior to defecating on him. (Are you shitting me? That's disgusting.)

In-Call—the agency or independent escort has a hotel room already paid for. Or the agency refers the client to a hotel that charges by the hour. Independents may also use their own residence as an in-call.

Independent—an escort who is not working for an agency and is responsible for marketing herself through various channels.

Injection Erection/Caverject—the use of a needle by the client to ensure his penis will be rock hard for hours. (A prolonged working hour for the escort.)

Jonesing—a client who has an intense craving for a party favor being delivered by an escort. (The son of a bitch keeps calling the dispatcher every five minutes.)

LFK—acronym for light French kissing.

K9—rear-entry sexual intercourse. (Definitely not referring to canines.)

K Hole—a client who is using ketamine and is lost in his own world. (Presumably a good idea for the escort to get the hell out of the call.)

Out-Call—the escort will go to the client's residence, hotel, car, boat, place of business, booth at the restaurant (after hours, of course), store at the strip center, etc.

Party Call—a request by the client to a dispatcher for a girl who will partake in using drugs during the call. The nature of the drug is sometimes communicated. Cocaine (soft) is the most commonly used drug on party calls.

Party Favors—an escort who carries drugs or can obtain them for a party call.

Party Girl—an experienced party girl will sit for hours with the client until she has collected all his money and enjoyed all of his party favors.

Patron Saint of Prostitutes—none other than old Saint Nick, who ironically paid to prevent two women from being prostitutes.

Peekers—a client who is high and paranoid and constantly peeking out his windows. (Remember, just because you're paranoid doesn't mean someone is not out to get you.)

Pre Ops/TS—also known as a "chick with a dick." Always independent, never with an agency. (Nothing personal, but never in my car under any circumstances.)

Private Call—an escort will do a call without booking it through the agency, thereby keeping all the proceeds.

Prostitute—synonyms include bawd, b-girl, call girl, concubine, courtesan, escort, fallen woman, fancy woman, good time girl, harlot, hoe, hustler, jezebel, lady of the evening, lady in red, lewd woman, loose woman, painted woman, sex worker, scarlet woman, street-walker, strumpet, tart, tramp, whore, working girl.

PSE—acronym for porn star experience. Porn actresses are common as visiting guests in strip clubs throughout the area, but a rare find in the escort business.

Raw Dick—coitus (sexual intercourse) without a condom. (The majority of clients are willing to pay extra for the opportunity.)

Sneakers—a client who is high, paranoid, and constantly sneaking around the walls and rooms of his own house.

Soft—a) a reference used by the client regarding the use or purchase of powder cocaine; b) a remark often used by escorts regarding a partying client who has not used a little blue pill or an injection.

Spinner—a term used by clients referring to a petite woman. (The possibility of her spinning like a top while sitting on your penis is physiologically impossible.)

Street-walkers—a prostitute, not an escort, who walks the streets. If she looks good, she's probably an undercover cop. (If in doubt, always ask to see her breasts before negotiating. If she suspects you're a cop, be prepared to whip out your penis.)

Strap On—an anal dildo used to penetrate the presumably bisexual male client. Escorts may keep one in the driver's trunk, so they can book the call.

Stuck in the Mirror—a strange phenomenon whereby an escort under the influence of drugs spends an extended period of time in the client's bathroom obsessing over her face. (The result is usually a frustrated client.)

Trip to the Islands—otherwise known as speaking Greek. A request by the client to a dispatcher for a girl who will partake in anal sex. This usually costs at least $100 above the agreed-upon rate, and deservedly, the C note is kept by the escort.

Tweakers—a client who is very high on methamphetamine, very agitated, and extremely restless.

She's at
YOUR
DOOR

ONE

South Florida Escort Industry

The South Florida escort industry is similar to escort services in any major city. Basically, you call an agency, and an escort shows up at your desired location. Escorts working in South Florida typically service Dade, Broward, and Palm Beach counties. To be even more specific, the agencies will send a girl from Homestead to Jupiter whenever possible. If a client pays with a credit card or is a regular, there is no telling where an escort will go. According to a number of escort agency owners, business is down at least one-third from seven years ago. The housing market collapse has taken a financial toll on the hooker industry. Fortunately for South Florida, we have a constant influx of vacationers and snowbirds. Typically, the winter months are the most profitable.

In the Guide to Acronyms & Terminology, I made mention of two specific types of escorts: those who work for an agency and those who are independent. My primary focus will be on the escorts who work for an agency and use my talents as a driver. A number of services allow escorts to drive themselves to calls, but only if the strumpets give the agency a two or three hundred dollar deposit. At every opportunity, I mention to the hookers the disadvantages of driving oneself. Even with a GPS navigation system, the ladies driving are prone to blowing calls by getting lost. Finding a parking space can also be a problem, and time is always of the essence. A large majority of calls involve alcohol or drugs. If a girl stays on a three-hour party call, she will no doubt be impaired. The money saved is soon forgotten when she is arrested for DUI and possibly drug possession. Even for the girl who has good navigation skills and is not a partier, there is the possibility of a physically abusive client. My presence alone usually discourages a man from attempting an acrimonious act. In actuality, using me as a driver is well worth the $25 per call I receive, despite the appeal of saving money.

This business of driving escorts is nothing like our forefathers could have imagined. Street-walking prostitutes and those in a whorehouse or brothel were but two ways men could enjoy their sexual fantasies in the past. Now, the escorts are delivered right to your front door (or back door if you prefer).

A search of South Florida escort websites is a favorite pursuit when requesting a lady. Clients may also call escort agencies featured in free adult magazines (located in strip clubs and swinger clubs) and free papers (no names, of course) found throughout the tricounty area. On rare occasions, the phone book will suffice. Even if a client has selected from a picture, it is doubtful she will be the woman knocking on his door. As a driver, it frustrates me to no end to see an attractive escort rejected because the client is fixated on a picture of a woman who was digitally created. There have been times I have convinced a client to accept a woman he has not selected. The girls are pestered when the dispatcher tells them to use a name from the website or magazine, pretending to be the requested woman. There are a limited number of agencies that do not partake in the bait-and-switch tactic; I have worked for three of them. One agency posted face and body pictures, another agency clouded the faces. The most recent service I worked for posted tastefully nude pictures. The truth of the matter is, if the guy opens the door and finds her appealing, her alias or professional name becomes irrelevant. (The majority of johns are usually under the influence, horny as shit, and any piece of ass will do.)

TWO

Ladies of the Evening

Anyone who has ever called an escort service knows escorts come in all ages, shapes, and nationalities. The girls in my car have ranged from seventeen to over forty, with the average age being twenty-four. The younger girls, if they are attractive, will book a greater amount of calls than the older ones. I personally have driven over one hundred escorts while working for the various escort services. One of the agencies I currently work for has close to 120 different girls working throughout the year. On average I may have thirty-five different girls riding in my car. More than half of these ladies of the evening will not be welcomed into my car for a second time. It could be for a nasty attitude, but more likely it's because they waste my time and gas when they consistently get rejected because of their unattractiveness.

I am often asked, "Are the girls hot?" Actually, the opposite is true: most of the girls are revolting. I wouldn't even buy them a drink if I were wearing tequila goggles. From an owner's standpoint, it would be ideal if every escort were a perfect ten, as there would be no calls lost due to rejection. Even in that case, 25 percent of clients would not be serviced because the elite escorts of any agency will respectfully decline a call to an unsafe neighborhood. Rather than lose the call, the agency will send an average girl who might actually book it.

If I pick up a girl for the first time, it is my job to screen her for the agency. Not long ago, I was instructed to pick up a woman from a hotel who called the service to begin working. When she opened the door, I immediately knew she didn't have "the look" to be a successful escort. (Let's not beat around the bush—she was fugly). I called up the owner who was dispatching and gave her the bad news. I didn't have the heart to tell the young lady, so I allowed her to stay in the car for a few hours before dropping her off.

So who are these ladies who are appealing to some men, repulsive to others, and without question, hated by most women? Each girl has her own sui generis story that led her down this avenue in life. The majority of them come from dysfunctional homes, where verbal, mental, and even physical abuse was the norm. Quite often, their home lives exposed them to the destructive nature of drugs and alcohol. A high percentage of working girls were molested and/or raped at an early age. Almost all were sexually active by the age of sixteen, if not sooner.

Why do these women run the risk of getting diseases, beaten, raped, robbed, or even killed? As one escort so aptly put it, "I'm in it for the money, honey." Although some women loathe being an escort, they have a chance to make an exceptional night's pay if they are reasonably attractive and the agency is busy. If a hooker is hot, she can work a four-day week and pocket $2,000 tax-free. The ladies also have the opportunity to work at their own leisure. On occasion, the escort can even refuse a call, should they feel uncomfortable. With unemployment hovering around 10 percent in South Florida, a single mom who has been unemployed for an extended period of time may be interested in working for an agency. There are also times a woman has to make a painful choice because her boyfriend either went to jail or has abandoned her. Based on my experience, more than half the escorts have a live-in boyfriend who is content to pimp her out. (South Florida seems to have an endless supply of dead beats.) Escorts often prevaricate about working for an agency by introducing me as a driver for the strip club they supposedly work for. Of course, the nonexistent strip club is usually in another county, so the boyfriend will be reluctant to come and see her dance.

A number of women work because they have to pay the court for probation costs or restitution money within a specific time or be sent back to prison. It is not uncommon for girls in my car to have warrants out for a previous prostitution charge or a drug-related charge. Fortunately, no woman has ever been arrested for drug possession, a warrant violation, or in a police sting while driving with me.

A number of girls working for the service are escorts because they are supporting their own drug addiction. (I like the 90/90 rule: 90 percent are addicts and 90 percent of their earnings go toward drugs). The preferred drugs of choice are Roxicodone (blues) and Xanax (bars). These two pills, which are commonly known as a drug cocktail, have replaced the crack cocaine that 90 percent of the escorts were abusing six years ago. Of all the girls riding in my car during the past two years, only one of them actually smoked crack. (Even the best perfume cannot cover up the fetid smell of crack.)

There are unusual circumstances through which a woman can enter the sordid world of sex for money. One woman who owned a cleaning service was exceptionally curious about being a call girl. I told her she would have to be in my car until the sun rose, and should she be arrested, she might be forced to forfeit her green card. One hour later, before her first call, I dropped her off at her home. One born-again Christian was so destitute she would pray and ask for God's forgiveness after each call. I tried to console her by letting her know Jesus understood her predicament.

The most important quality an escort can possess, from a financial perspective, is the ability to extend the call. (This is referred to as "she has game.") In most cases, the hours go by while the client and the escort party the night away. Nonetheless, the escort must be coherent so she can collect and check in every hour. It is inevitable that an escort will become disarrayed and lose track of time. When she calls me, I am expected to apprise her of the exact time she can leave the client. As a professional, it is imperative I keep very accurate time and money records in my notebook. Here is a sample of my daily call sheet:

Location	Time	Amount	Drop	My Take	Ladies' Take

There are moneymakers who do not have game. They go to a call, collect the money, make the guy happy, and depart as quickly as possible. One seductive escort had it down to a science: after collecting the fee, she immediately "wakes it up" by performing oral sex—with a condom, of course. The gentleman was then allowed to request up to three coitus positions. If he was still unsuccessful, she jack-hammered him with her hand. The last resort for the john was for him to use his own hand while she pretended to masturbate. All of this was done within a fifty-minute window period, known as the "escort hour." (If you are unable to cum in fifty minutes, the other ten minutes probably just adds to the frustration.)

A john is only allowed one ejaculation in the hour, so if it happens in the first five minutes, then the hour is up. (If you're a quick popper, I recommend more foreplay.) Should the client want a second round ("multiple cups"), he can either negotiate the price with the dispatcher for a second hour or offer the girl a nice tip so she feels inclined to stay longer during the initial hour. Although it is sometimes referred to as a date, the escort has one thing on her mind: the money she will collect on her next call. There are times an escort will have an orgasm, but this is the exception to the rule. (When does a hooker come twice? Once when she collects the money and the other is when she is spending it.) Almost all call girls use condoms for intercourse, about twenty five percent will only perform a CBJ. If the service is marketing their escort's as GFE then she is expected to comply with a BBBJ. Condoms present a problem for the over-fifty age group, as this group has a natural tendency to be desensitized. Clients sometimes offer a considerable amount of money if they can ride bareback while having intercourse with the escort. This can be very tempting for a woman who is desperate for money. I have actually driven young ladies who are not aware of the inherent risks of not using a condom. It is hard to believe that some girls (usually young and dumb) do not realize they can get AIDS if the guy is infected and ejaculates inside them. One of my regular escorts had a very convincing line when addressing a client's desire to have sex without a condom: "I have respect for myself, and you need to have respect for me."

Since the majority of escorts do not use any form of birth control, there is ample opportunity for them to get pregnant should the condom break. I remember one night when an escort was understandably very upset because the client ejaculated and neither realized the condom had broken. Escorts can and do complain about having too much sex in a given night. Most escorts call it a night after having sex with the fifth guy. One exceptional older escort, who always carried a small travel bag filled with numerous gels and creams, had no problem doing eight different guys on her shift. It is rare to find an escort who will have sex with more than one male at a time, even if both johns have paid. The idea of being gang-banged is more suitable for swingers than escorts.

I have driven strippers who prefer escorting to dancing simply because it is more intimate and less degrading. (No doubt, it is debasing getting on one's knees to pick up dollar bills thrown on the stage when her set is finished.)

There are escorts who have been in the business for fifteen years, but it is difficult to know who will make a career of it. I have yet to meet a woman who was escorting to finance her college tuition. They bullshit themselves and each other about going to college. At times, an escort will actually enjoy going to a particular client, usually for one of two reasons: he is either a good tipper and will extend, or he has her drug of choice. There are a handful of escorts who actually became romantically involved with the agency owners. It is common for the drivers and occasionally the dispatchers to become sexually involved with the escorts. Recently, an escort I was driving for six months married a rich john. She might have paid him $10,000, which is the going rate for a foreigner to stay in America when their visas expire. As for escorts being swept off their feet by a client, good luck with the *Pretty Woman* scenario because it rarely happens.

THREE

Hooker Bookers

The most troublesome position to fill for any agency is that of a dispatcher. Phone managers, as they are sometimes called, need to be steadfast for up to twelve hours. Considering South Florida has a diverse population with a number of languages spoken, being bilingual in English and Spanish is essential, especially when dealing with clients from Dade County. In Florida's busy season, a prosperous agency may require two dispatchers on a Friday or Saturday night. As a former dispatcher, I was always comfortable talking to clients about finding the right woman to satisfy their sexual desires. I felt it was my obligation to let the clients in on whether a particular escort was a good lay or not.

As for female dispatchers, they better have thick skin. Occasionally, perverted men will call escort agencies with the desire to converse in a sexually explicit manner so they can masturbate. The jury is out on whether a male dispatcher is capable of booking more calls than a female with equal abilities.

What makes dispatching so challenging is not just

excluding the sexual degenerates (previously mentioned), pranksters (who have nothing better to do), and the time wasters (who fantasize, but won't spend the money), but sending the ideal escort to the call. If the dispatcher is employed by a service that does not use bait-and-switch, there is a high probability the call will go through. There is, however, one more element the phone manager has to consider when setting up the call. Is the guy on the phone a police officer who is part of a hotel/condo sting operation? With at least fifteen escort agencies in the tricounty area, a seasoned dispatcher quickly realizes the significance of building an ongoing phone relationship with clients. The escort business is no different from any other sales profession: people buy from people they like. To succeed, it is necessary for the dispatcher to develop an understanding of the client's desires on any given night. Of course, hooker availability plays an important role in fulfilling the john's sexual appetite.

Each agency will have a potential escort fill out an application similar to the one on the following page.

As a dispatcher, there were two reasons I wanted to meet the girls personally: most importantly, to see if they were appealing (were they hotter than their Internet picture?), and to ask them specific questions regarding the Do's and Don'ts.

Questions such as: "Do you do party calls?" and "Are you racist?" and "Are you comfortable doing a couple call?" The answers are preeminent to future booking possibilities. Sending a straight hooker on a couple call is a huge mistake. When an escort is rejected, there is lost

Application for Employment as Independent Contractor

Real Name _____ Work Name _____

Age _____ Date of Birth _____

Address _____ City _____

State _____ Zip _____

Home Phone_____ Cell Phone_____

Email _____

Driver License # _____ State _____

Exp. _____ Social Security # _____

How did you hear about us? _____

Height _____ Weight _____ Bust/Cup_____

Hair Color _____ Eye Color _____ Nationality _____

Do you have access to a car?_____ Year/Make_____

What languages, besides English, do you speak?_____

Have you ever worked for an escort agency? _____

If yes, who have you worked for?_____

Are you currently registered with another agency?_____

Is your home or other place available for client visits?_____

If yes, what is the address?_____

What shifts do you want to work?   Days_____ Evenings_____

Do you want us to include your picture in our advertising?_____

DO's_____

DON'Ts_____

Name_____ Signature_____

revenue for the company, as well as credibility with the client for future services. (The bait-and-switch service I worked for had over thirty phone numbers with several advertised names and didn't give a shit about integrity.)

Obviously, dispatchers who work for companies that do not use bait-and-switch will inevitably have fewer rejections. Escorts working for agencies which advertise on the website www.independentgirls.com also known as the Indi-Board, have an opportunity to establish a loyal customer base by getting a review like the one below:

Jillian has been reviewed a number of times already, so basically I am just piling on, but my main point in writing this is to let you guys know that she is still delivering a top-notch GFE+ experience. She opened the door to the in-call and greeted me wearing a sexy bra and panties and a big smile. She looks like her pictures, she has a beautiful face, and her body is superb. Her ass is something to die for. Nice tits and soft smooth skin. We got comfortable, all the while engaging in small talk. Some LFK commenced, and that gradually turned into DFK as the date's intensity began to heat up.

She enjoys touching and caressing and also enjoys the same in return. After licking her nice tits and nipples, I proceeded to DATY. She was already wet and very responsive to everything I did to her. Next she began to service my tool with some excellent BBBJ, very DT [deep throat], almost putting the entire tool in the shed, but left a small amount outside. She also introduced herself to my boys [testicles] and made sure they were having a good time as well . . . and they were. I enjoyed this for a while and then she brought out some covers [condoms].

This was ok because I was ready to move on to the FS. The main event was a blur of 69, mish [missionary], doggie [girl whose on all fours], cg [cow girl], rcg [reverse cow girl], you name it. She served up cookies [orgasms] at least three times, YMMV [your mileage may vary]. It was too much for Mr. Happy, and he let it loose. Afterwards we kissed and caressed for a while. The whole experience was unrushed and was like being with a true girlfriend. I know a lot of ladies claim to be GFE and really aren't. I can assure you that this was the best GFE experience I've ever had. She was a willing and enthusiastic participant during our date. She was not afraid to suggest things and was not opposed to try anything within reason. IMHO, she made it abundantly clear that she enjoys sex, and she basically surrendered herself to me for one hour. Dirty talk was also sprinkled in here and there during the date. She wants you to be satisfied when you leave, and, believe me, I was.

P.S. Two cups were offered [the john could cum twice in the hour], and Greek is available for an extra donation.

Although most dispatchers get paid an hourly wage, they receive a bonus after booking a thousand dollars on their shift. Rather than lose any calls, deceitful phone managers working for bait-and-switch agencies use a number of techniques that occasionally may be successful.

1. The dispatcher may send an escort who looks nothing like the fabricated girl in the picture.

2. The dispatcher will send the closest escort regardless of what the client has asked for.

3. The dispatcher will tell the clients an escort will be there
in a half-hour when they know for a fact it may be an
hour or more.

There are unscrupulous dispatchers who send repugnant
escorts to a call, knowing she will provide the phone manager with a tip should she actually service the customer.
Should the owner of an escort company find out a dispatcher is steering certain girls for money or receiving sexual favors, he will be fired immediately.

Apathetic phone operators are those who have a blatant
disregard for the safety of both the drivers and escorts. On
occasion, they will attempt to call a hooker out of the
client's house early in order to book another call. While
they are sitting in an air-conditioned office miles away, all
hell is breaking loose as the pissed-off client is chasing the
half-naked escort out of the house while demanding his
money back.

One of the agencies I am working for now will not allow
you inside the office at any time. Previously, drivers and
escorts were allowed to relax on leather couches and watch
television antecedent to their next call. A policy change was
necessary after an assailant strong-armed the owner and
purloined the cash on hand. There is little doubt one of the
hookers was in on the heist, as there were a number of security cameras outside and inside. After that incident, it was
decided that all drivers and escorts when making the drop
would hand the money to the dispatcher through a slot in
the glass door. It is not uncommon for drivers and dispatchers to clash. One such occurrence escalated when a driver

returned to the office and sucker-punched the dispatcher. He fulfilled a fantasy many men have considered on their last day of work. Of course there were no repercussions; surely the phone manager wasn't going to call the police.

A couple of months later, a phone manager locked himself out of the office when he went outside to converse with a hooker. Even though the cameras could be viewed at the owner's residence (she lived ten minutes away), the dispatcher idiotically shattered the front window to regain entrance and resume answering the phones. No surprise, it was his last day of work.

Surprisingly, even the most seasoned dispatchers do not authenticate the room number where the client is calling from when booking a hotel call. The phone manager should get the last name of the client; call the hotel front desk, and have them transfer the call. When the john answers the phone he is confirming that he actually called the agency and the room number is correct. There are other consequences besides lost time and gas when pursuing bogus hotel calls. Once, there was a call to an upscale motel at 4 A.M. When the escort knocked on the door, a baby started crying and the rest of the family awoke. Apparently, the slothful glutton of a phone manager never bothered to validate the room number.

There have been occasions I have had my differences with phone managers. One winter night, I received a call from a dispatcher and put the address in my GPS, only to have it malfunction and freeze up. I repeatedly tried plugging in the address, until I called the dispatcher and he gave me the client's number so I could speak to him directly. The client insisted the address was correct, but I knew he was full of shit. It turned out to be a bogus call, and the caller was knowingly setting up drivers who were using this navigation system. The dispatcher refused to accept the simple fact that the asshole was playing all of us, and we had a contentious conversation over the phone.

One slow Friday night, I almost got fired by one of the agencies I worked for. The owner expected me to go to local strip clubs and put the agency's business cards on the windshields of parked cars. I refused to go on private property and risk getting arrested and possibly assaulted by the bouncers. I remember telling the girls in my car, "What the hell is she thinking, I'm trying to keep a low profile and she is putting us in harm's way?"

On a hot humid Saturday night, I took three girls to a regular client's mansion in Boca Raton. He would normally take at least two escorts at a time and switch them out. At the end of four hours we departed, only to find that the client had called the office complaining his wallet was missing. Normally, the phone manager couldn't give a shit, but because the client was a profitable regular, the situation needed to be investigated. Unfortunately, I found myself in a quandary. Although two of the girls had a reputation for pilfering, there was a very good possibility the client might have been in a K-hole and misplaced his wallet. At the urging of the dispatcher, I took the ladies to a local convenience store where they had to empty all of their personal belongings. I didn't expect to find the wallet or the money. If one of them did take it, she would have taken the money out and ditched the wallet. All hookers have mastered the "pussy hideaway technique" and I certainly wasn't in the mood to go exploring. A month later, I returned to the South American client's stately home and was greeted in the driveway. As the escort was getting out of the car, he handed me a $100 tip and informed me that he had found his wallet—but one of the tramps had lifted his watch.

There was one exceptional Brazilian dispatcher who I worked with for a year. He was so proficient at booking calls that I worked on his schedule, driving the nights he worked and relaxing when he didn't. One night after I checked in with the first call, I could tell he was extremely disconcerted. He accused me of telling the owner that he would only give calls to drivers/escorts if they tipped him cash or cocaine (which was commonly used to stay alert through one's shift). Although this was actually true, knowing the owner's antidrug policy, I wouldn't dream of condemning my cash cow. I never knew who falsely accused me, but after numerous calls, I finally convinced the phone manager of the logical fact: it would not be in my best interest to cut off my only source of income. A couple of nights later, the owner called me and asked if I knew where he was. She was concerned he might have taken another job and was going to ask me to switch agencies as well. Truth be told, he simply vanished.

FOUR

Tramps in Transit

A number of experienced escorts have said to me, "You're a perfect fit for this job." As a nocturnal individual, I always function better between 10 P.M. and 4 A.M. My reputation as one of the top drivers is directly related to never driving under the influence of drugs or alcohol. With over a million miles under my belt, the escorts feel completely at ease with my driving style and my knowledge of the tricounty area. I am always professional and courteous to the clients, whether in person or on the phone. In case I am pulled over, I have a mature, clean-cut look, and all my automotive paperwork is up to date. Even with a clean driving and arrest record, it is imperative I remain cool, calm, and collected regardless of the circumstances.

Growing up on the streets of the Bronx provided me with the ability to think on my feet and sense trouble before it happens. Although I did make a mistake one night in Snapper Creek, when three escorts came out of a call loudly complaining that one of the johns had venereal warts. Understandably, she didn't perform any services nor did she return the money, having already checked in. Despite my sense of urgency regarding the impending consequences of walking out on a call, she preferred to smoke a cigarette—that is, until seven furious Cuban guys exited the residence. I should have made a u-turn when she got in the car, but I passed by the house not realizing the johns were going to hurl metal objects at my car. The damage was minimal, but it was her last night working for the agency.

Contrary to other escort drivers in the business, I treat the ladies with dignity and I expect the same in return. When we have a call in a townhouse community, I am one of the few chauffeurs who will protectively stroll with an escort until we find the john's address. (Of course, this only applies if she is good earner.) However, there were two situations where it was necessary for me to verbally remove undignified ladies from my car. I am considerate with the escorts and their numerous requests, yet I am firm when it comes to business. At the beginning of the night, I always emphasize the reason they're in my car: "To make money." I have two rules I expect the escorts to follow: don't cheat me out of my money and no smoking in the car. The escorts know that if they smoke, they need to spray perfume or body spray before reentering the hooker mobile. I also have no tolerance for escorts who are incapable of servicing the client because they are intoxicated or wasted.

As for the escorts carrying and doing drugs throughout the evening, every situation is unique. Many drivers have been asked to make party-favor runs, either by the escort's connection or the dispatcher. One of the escorts working for the agency lived with a coke dealer and always had five $40 dollar bags in her possession. She was great at extending, and of course, she made money on the sale of cocaine as well.

There are times when a driver is asked to perform unusual tasks. While servicing her clients, one sexy escort actually had me babysit Louie, her Chihuahua. The evening was uncharacteristically cold, and the adorable dog came prepared with a blanket, pillow, and doggie sweater. If a client needs to use the local ATM, I am always willing to drive him for a $20 fee. (If he can afford to spend a couple hundred bucks on a whore, then he can pay me extra for making it possible.)

I have been asked a number of times to go into an all-night pharmacy and purchase soft cups, sponges, or triangular make-up pads. For those not in the business, these are used when an escort gets her period and still needs to continue to work. Bleeding on a call is embarrassing for the escort, and clients usually become enraged. I have even taken escorts for their gynecological examinations and to purchase their birth control pills.

As is necessary for all driving professionals, one needs to be prepared for their occupation. I carry a simple indispensable Hooker Kit, including:

- GPS: You would be a fool not to use one.

- SunPass: Sometimes, two minutes can make all the difference.

- Large box of condoms: For those moments when you arrive at the client's house in the middle of nowhere and the escort thought she had one.

- Counterfeit pen: To catch a thief.

- Pen and pad: Necessary for entering information on my daily call sheet.

- Calculator: Quite useful when an escort has just left a five-hour party call. The hooker will foolishly use her fingers to determine how much she keeps and how much goes to the office.

- Flashlight: Necessary for the girls to continually find their misplaced possessions.

- Cell phone power chargers: A driver should possess the standard two chargers. The ladies will inevitably forget their own charger and kill their battery early in the evening.

- Vomit supplies (plastic barf bag, paper towels, unopened bottle of water, gum, and body spray): For the ladies who can't control the intoxicating substances they have ingested throughout the evening.

Additional supplies include:

- Pillow (for the long nights)

- Blanket (for the rare cold ones)

- Shorts and T-shirt (evening to morning calls)

- Beach chair and bathing suit (evening to morning calls with a nearby beach)

The first agency I worked for had the drivers call the office between 5 and 6 P.M. to get the addresses of the escorts they were picking up. There are other agencies where you sit in the office with the escorts until there is a call. The last two agencies I worked for did not require the drivers to work on a fixed schedule. You could call any escort working for the agency or she could call you to drive her on any given night. The freedom to work when it is convenient is usually only afforded to escorts, not drivers. Having worked with this agency for over a year, I have over thirty escorts listed in my phone. For eight months, I drove a beautiful, exotic Brazilian/Chinese woman. Fortunately, she was friendly with the other escorts who had the privilege to ride in the car with her.

During the week we worked alone, but on the weekends she allowed other escorts to ride in the back seat. Friday and Saturday nights were usually the money-makers and two-girl calls were more commonplace. There is a distinct advantage if you have two hot tramps riding with you. The dispatcher is more inclined to send you on a two-girl call. There have been occasions when I have driven three girls. The possibility of all three girls doing the same number of calls is highly unlikely. Thus, the bitching and moaning is not worth the few extra dollars. On average, with one girl on a busy night, I can walk away with $150–$200 cash, and that can double with two girls in the car.

When an escort who is new to the business secures a seat in my car, I feel it is my responsibility to prepare her for an engaging evening. Foremost, is her ability to communicate with me by paying attention to her phone during the call.

It may be necessary for the escort to finish quickly because there is a request for her at another location. Once in the call, time management and knowing when the hour is finished is crucial. The novice escort will ask me to call her on the half-hour. I reiterate the importance of tracking one's own time—even it means setting the alarm on her phone.

Once I have the escorts in the car, it is a waiting game until the dispatcher calls. The escorts keep themselves entertained, usually by texting. Quite often, the hookers will happily take out their expensive phones and show me naked pictures of themselves or their colleagues.

When we do get a call, there are a number of questions that have to be answered either directly or indirectly for the escort to check in:

- Is it a prank call?

- Will the client have the money?

- Will the client be awake or change his mind when you arrive?

- Has the client called another agency?

- Is the girl in the car a good fit?

- Will the client only accept the girl from the picture?

One of the companies I am working for now will only provide the driver with the client's address for their GPS. When I arrive at a location, the price, room number, and whether the request is for more than one girl is disclosed. This procedure of withholding information is designed so the driver/girl do not steal the call. There are at least two other methods to do a call and not pay the office. The first can be used when driving two escorts and the call is in a remote area or it is a very slow night. After one of the girls checks in, she will try to convince the client to bring the other escort into the call for a two-girl show at a discounted rate. This subterfuge can get complicated should the driver get another call twenty minutes later. A number of drivers have been fired when the second escort doesn't come out quickly enough for the next call.

The other method to defraud the agency is much easier to accomplish. On the last call of the evening, an escort will check in for the first hour as is customary. Even if the client is extending, I call the office and check her out. To avoid suspicion, I have the escorts come back to the car and say goodnight to the dispatcher. Quite often, the hookers will have money in hand and be wearing his shirt and sandals. Leaving her clothes behind ensures the john she will return. The escort will keep all the money, but she now has to pay me $50 an hour. I will call the office and sign off, letting the office know we are going to stop for breakfast. If the call continues into the third hour, I will go back to the office and make the drop. One morning, the last call was very close to the office and it was necessary for me to bring the reluctant escort back with the drop. If the dispatcher did not literally see her, he could charge her for the next hour. After a quick stop at the store, she returned for another four hours with the client. Another way to make extra cash while working with some agencies is to make up an excuse to call off earlier than expected and do private calls. There have even been times when I pick up one or two of my regular girls and we only do private calls.

As a driver, I like to briefly show my presence at the individual's house. I will typically be backing out of the driveway slowly as the escort knocks on the door. In this way, the client sees she has a bodyguard, and yet I am respecting his privacy by not parking in his driveway or in front of his house. In gated communities, I always park and wait at the community pool. Should the escort be in an onerous situation and I have exited the community, I will not be in a position to render her assistance (drivers have been known to use patio furniture to break a window to gain entry). When I am not in a community, the closest strip mall will suffice. Between calls, I prefer to wait in the parking lot of a twenty-four-hour eating establishment. If we are not dining in, it is prudent to purchase a beverage, which will have a printed logo on it. One escort termed this the "alibi cup."

Hotel calls have a unique protocol. I usually drive around the parking lot with the escort while surveying the cars looking for a police presence. One of my regular escorts prefers I walk her through the hotel lobby to the actual floor where the client's room is located. This was a common practice at my first agency where I had to collect the money from the clients. I developed a system whereby the escort would enter the hotel room, collect the money, and stick only the money out the door for me to accept. This procedure of minimizing my presence eliminates the client's fear of an undercover sting and the potential for a "cash 'n' dash" scenario. I always remind the escorts to be vigilant for a possible sting operation every time we arrive at a hotel. When she encounters a client, it behooves her to look for luggage in the room and ask if she may glance at his plane ticket.

One night I was driving an attractive, large-breasted Columbian escort who had been arrested a couple of months earlier in a prostitution sting. When we arrived at the North Miami Beach condo, we were greeted by a very sober, clean-cut, and extremely friendly individual. As she was exiting the car, he asked me, "How does this work?" I immediately called her back to the car and explained to the gentleman that there must have been a mistake and I needed to check with the office. I am not 100 percent sure he was undercover, but by every indication he played the part. The escort felt the same way and was grateful I had her best interests in mind.

Unfortunately, on a torpid Saturday night, I drove this same escort to a call in Hollywood where all hell broke loose. As I arrived at the hotel, I was approached by a couple of young Southern gentlemen. One client was enamored with the sexy hooker and handed me the cash before they proceeded to his room. After the hour was finished, she called me to get a price on the hourly rate for the next eight hours. (Depending on the dispatcher, a multiple-hour call may be discounted.) While awaiting a call back, I was informed by his buddy that this young hobbyist had a propensity for spending all his money on hookers when he was on vacation. As I waited with the other tramp outside the hotel, the Colombian escort came frantically running to the car, saying, "The police are coming!"

Apparently two of the john's friends had arrived at the hotel, realized he had broken his pact not to call any escorts on this vacation, and unbelievably, they called the authorities. Not wanting to lose an all-night call, we drove up the street and waited to see if the police would arrive. As we passively waited, the shirtless john left his friends in the room and came over to the car. When the police appeared, he jumped in my car and asked to be taken to another hotel. As I was about to leave the area, the escort started yelling so loudly (totally freaking out) that the police actually heard her and looked in our direction before heading into the hotel. She continued to scream hysterically as I made a u-turn and left the area.

After a few quick turns, I thought we may have averted a calamity and would complete the lucrative call. However, it wasn't meant to be, because, still visibly trembling, the escort who completed the initial call demanded I pull over and let her out. The topless john also left my car and chased her across the street, still hoping to get a room. When I returned to the office in the early morning hours, the owner thought the escort was trying to steal the call with this melodramatic escapade. Eventually, both of us came to the conclusion that the hooker's overreaction at the mere presence of law officers was based on her recent arrest for the solicitation of prostitution.

Anonymity is the best defense for the driver and escort regarding the authorities. I frequently tell the girls, "I am always in the wrong place at the wrong time." In one instance, a foolish driver actually called attention to his car by parking between two palm trees in the divider of a road.

When the Kendall police arrived, they thought he had hit one of the trees. When questioned, he panicked, told the officers he was an escort driver, and gave them the address where he dropped off the hooker. They knocked on the john's door, ran a background check, and she was arrested for an outstanding warrant.

There is the belief by the majority of escorts that their driver will protect them should a threatening situation occur. Here's a reality check: if the client is carrying a weapon, on steroids, or enraged, it's time to call 911. As one urban driver put it: "Hoe, you're on your own till the Man shows up."

The following is from a handout that was given to me on my very first night as an escort driver. As you can see, there is no mention of protecting the escorts; it is just an implied responsibility.

PLEASE REVIEW THESE POINTS WITH NEW POTENTIAL DRIVERS

1. The driver is to provide in addition to proper identifi-cation: dependable cell phone with cigarette lighter power charger, counterfeit pen, fold out maps for Dade, Broward, and Palm Beach Counties. It is expected that the driver will keep an eye on signal strength at all times. It is vital that we are able to reach a driver. It is also advisable to have a back-up beeper just in case. Try to keep your phone on your dash or close to a window.

2. Drivers are to call in by 6:15 P.M. for assignments; escorts are to be picked up between 7:30–8:00 P.M.

3. If there are no calls at the time of pick-up, the driver is to wait close to I-95 until called. Coffee shops such as Java Cup are perfect for waiting. NO BARS! The escorts are to stay with you or at least be within driver's sight at all times. You may wait five minutes or you might be waiting three hours for your first call. You are to remain in the same area or within one exit of I-95. If you wish to go beyond that area, you must contact the office first. ETAs given to customers are based on where the dispatcher knows the driver to be at any given time.

4. If escorts do not do any calls, the driver does not make any money.

5. We work until 6:00 A.M., seven days a week. No exceptions whatsoever! It is possible that a call may go later than expected, thus keeping a driver out even later. No family emergencies are considered. If the escort says she is sick, she can be taken to the hospital at the discretion of the office. Proof of medical services will be required or the escort will be fined. It is also expected of the driver to help encourage the escort to continue working even after her 6:00 A.M. shift is over.

6. Pay is $25.00 per completed call. Calls are at least one hour. If escorts go multiple hours, driver is paid $25.00 per hour. After the first hour, we accept additional half hours for which the driver will be paid $12.50. The fee of $25.00 is the same whether the call is $180 or $300 per hour. While drivers are often tipped by the escorts, it is not required. No tips should be expected. If booking is with credit card, driver is paid $31.50 per call per hour instead of $25.00; the pay period for credit card calls ends on Saturday and is paid the following Friday. Driver is responsible for checking accuracy and completion of charge slips. It cannot be emphasized enough how important it is to do a complete, clean, and clear credit card imprint. All fees (cash or credit) are collected by the driver when escort arrives. The office will elaborate during the interview and instruct the driver for credit card procedures. All money and credit card slips are to be kept in a safe and locked place, such as a car trunk or glove compartment until the end of the shift or until the office instructs driver where and to whom to drop to. Driver is responsible for all cash and credit card slips. Driver is also responsible for counterfeit bills. All bills should be checked with a counterfeit pen before accepting money either from pick-ups or customers. If you collect a counterfeit bill, you'll know who it came from and notify the office immediately. DO NOT KEEP MONEY ON YOUR PERSON AND DO NOT PAY ESCORT UNTIL THE END OF YOUR SHIFT!

7. In addition to the $25.00 fee, the driver makes an additional $10.00 per escort per evening for collection of

cash and charge slips. When another driver/employee of the service collects money, the driver will pay $10.00 to the person making the collection. This is $10.00 per collection, not $10.00 per girl. Collections are authorized by office directly to driver. The driver is not given a choice when or where to drop. The office always makes this determination.

8. It is important to remember that when starting out it is possible to go out on a shift and make little to nothing one night, then make quite a bit the next or even following evening. We usually work new drivers in slowly. If you're patient and dependable, you will do very well. This business has no set times of being busy or slow. While it is traditionally busier on weekends, it is also quite possible to make more money on a Monday than on a Saturday. Fraternization with the girls is not tolerated AT ALL. We do not want personal relationships to be established. It is bad for business. This includes the exchange of phone numbers and/or any rendezvous.

FIVE

At Your Door

A call can be in a swanky hotel in South Beach, a five-star resort in Palm Beach, or a dive motel anywhere in between. An escort may be lying on her back in a beautiful mansion on the ocean worth millions or in a back room rented as an apartment with a side entrance. The enigma is, unless he is a regular with the agency and his spending habits are known, nobody knows who the big spender will be on any given evening.

On a rare cold night I had two girls riding with me when we proceeded to a low-income area in downtown Miami. The client was literally hanging out on the curb and actually stood up so I could pull up. His residence was an apartment house for individuals who are in rehab. He ended up switching out the girls and spent over $1,500 during a seven-hour period. I am quick to inform the new girls that you never know what's in a man's pocket and how much he will spend, regardless of where he lives. If he exhibits a large amount of currency, then it is their purpose to relieve him of his cash by means of extending.

So what takes place once an escort is accepted by the john and enters the premises? Unless you are the hottest woman the client has ever seen, a relaxed attitude is paramount before collecting the money. She usually offers him a hug and a kiss as part of her introduction. Once the small talk ends, the escort will collect the fee. The fee with the agency I am currently working for is $150 to $300 per hour for an individual and $250 to $500 for a couple's call. The girl receives the first $100 and splits anything over $200 with the agency. I have worked for other agencies that take the first $100 and the escort receives the remaining cash. Before entering any location, the escort and the driver have been notified concerning the amount she needs to collect. On occasion, there might be a disagreement about the fee as the client tries to renegotiate the original price. On a slow night he might be successful, but never for less than $150. One escort had a technique for getting a larger tip by calling the office on the client's behalf, offering a lower price, and keeping the difference. The escort always collects the money up front, unless she is doing a private call to one of her regular clients she trusts. When the money is collected, she notifies the driver (checks in) and he, in turn, calls the agency. Many experienced escorts will call both for fear the driver will forget and the office may call her at an inopportune moment. I always prefer they check in with me so I know they are safe. To safeguard against robberies, the escorts who drive with me have a special code word they can use if they find themselves in a threatening situation. I, of course, immediately call 911 once the word is spoken.

I have driven escorts to over one thousand calls, and not one has ever been harmed physically. However, the low-lives and degenerates the escorts encounter can mentally take their toll. Recently, one of the escorts I was driving was supposedly robbed of $600. When I picked her up, she barred out in the car, only to awaken and claim her wallet was missing. This cunning technique is an effective way for the escort to keep all the money if she has no intention of working for the agency again.

Escorts can also be duped by inadvertently accepting counterfeit money. This took place when an experienced escort came out of the call and handed me four question-able $50 bills. The lighting was dark when she received the crumpled bills, and she didn't bother to look carefully at the money. Since the client left his home in the gated community at the same time I picked up the escort, there was no recourse. Even though the girl screwed up for accepting the bills, I would have made him pay the price in more ways than one. The escort had to pay the agency the $80 she owed, regardless of her unfortunate mistake. I felt sorry and waived my fee. The next day I contacted the Secret Service in an attempt to turn in the imperfect $50 bills and the sorry-ass counterfeiter. To my amaze-ment, they informed me that it was out of their jurisdiction and they recommended that I should *not* contact the Palm Beach County Sheriff's office. I was told "the circum-stances by which I came into possession of the money may cause problems for me." Although I took the advice, I did let the dispatcher know to blacklist the number the asshole used to call the agency. Two weeks later, the silver-haired

Boca Raton swindler had the audacity to the call the agency again.

The first agency I worked for was the only one I know of where the driver was required to collect the money from the clients. With over 450 girls working for him in a three-year period, the agency owner decided after the first year it was time to entrust the drivers. Prior to the change, there were numerous occasions in which new escorts, after being on an extended call, kept all the money by having a friend waiting at the back door of the hotel or residence. I took no satisfaction in meeting every john, nor were they pleased to make my acquaintance. I can say with earnest that the girls didn't book certain calls because I emphatically resemble a police officer. If the customer was paying cash, I found a way to make it profitable. The usual price for a one-hour call with this agency was $180, and if the customer handed me two $100 bills, I never had change. On a busy night, I would earn an extra $60 by not offering exact change.

The credit card process was comparatively time consuming. I first needed to see a driver's license to match the name on the credit card. While filling out the credit card slip, I would call the office and give the dispatcher the numbers on the credit card. The dispatcher would run the credit card to verify funds and tell me the authorization code to place on the credit card slip. After sliding the card through the machine, the client had to sign the credit card slip and sign a disclaimer similar to this:

The owner was very proud of the fact that, in over three years, only one customer with "hooker's remorse" managed

---

DISCLAIMER

I'm satisfied with any/all services rendered by Escorts Inc. and/or their agents. Furthermore, I hereby waive my right to any/all claims of any nature whatsoever that may arise as a result of this transaction/services in past, present, and future.

Furthermore, as a cardholder I acknowledge receipt of goods/services in the amount of $_____, the total shown herein and on the credit card receipt, and I agree to pay this obligation as set forth in the credit card cardholder's agreement with the issuer, and will not dispute or charge back this transaction for any reason.

Signature_____ Date_____

Printed Name_____

Driver's License No._____ State_____

Witness _____

to get his money back from the credit card company. (Imagine waking up with a splitting headache, having no clue what happened the night before, and seeing your signature on credit card slips amounting to thousands.) We could bill up to $2,500 on one card, but if you got a verification code off the back of the second credit card then you could bill up to three thousand. Once I collected the money or had the necessary paperwork signed, I would leave, call the office, and the client's hour would begin.

It is standard in the industry that the ladies of the evening will receive their share of the credit card transactions once a week. The most efficient way a call girl can retain accurate records is to take a picture of the client's credit card and license with her cell phone. Fastidious agencies require the escort to carry a finger print pad and she is expected to add the client's thumb print to the paper work. An adroit escort will purchase a square credit card reader, attach it to their smart phones, and have the gratuity directly deposited in her bank account. This prevents the agency from acquiring a percentage of the tip money. From a fallacious stand point, it is a common practice for agencies that accept credit cards to withhold the escort's share by fining them for minor infractions, giving them unsigned checks, and even issuing checks without bank routing numbers. Their attitude is: What's mine is mine, and what's yours is mine.

The average call is usually booked as one hour but takes, on average, only thirty-five minutes to complete. If she should go over the allotted time by fifteen minutes, she will have to pay the agency fee for a second hour. That's no problem if the guy is extending, but if he is not, it is a definite loss of revenue for the escort. I have a number of excuses I will tell the dispatcher to bail the escort's asses out.

An escort's ability to keep her phone nearby while in a call is imperative. I might receive a call from the dispatcher that a regular wants to see her for the next four hours. The client might be all coked up and will keep calling the dispatcher every ten minutes asking, "Where is she?"

I would never call her while she is in a call, but I will text her with information regarding her financial well-being. However, most dispatchers will call with an order to leave before the hour is up and place her in a confrontational situation with the client. The phone manager sometimes asks the hooker to blow out of one call so he can book her a multiple-hour call. There are calls where the john will pay for two hours or more up front. This can be problematic with a salacious escort who is more interested in money than customer satisfaction. On one such occasion, a regular client paid the escort for three hours up front. Not even fifteen minutes into the call, he goes to the bathroom, and when he comes out, he is the victim of a cash 'n' dash. He was infuriated when the agency refused to offer him a replacement or refund. Keep in mind, this was a regular client. Instead of having the girl return to the office with the money, the owner foolishly blew it off. At this time, the john no longer deals with the agency, but he will contact me when his ship is in port. He knows I will only deliver a girl he will find stimulating and wouldn't venture to take his money and run. I am always happy to drive any escorts to private calls. I receive $50 an hour per girl, plus my usual $20 for picking up the girl and driving her home. On a private call with two girls staying for two hours, I drive away with $240 tax free before tip. When a girl books a couple's call through the agency, the driver receives $50 an hour. Maybe twice a month, the escorts will do what is called a "girl on girl call" or a "couple call." In all likelihood, 80 percent of all escorts are bisexual and 10 percent are willing to fake it for the money. (It would be rather difficult for a straight guy to pretend to be bisexual regardless of the money involved.) Once the money is dealt with and the appropriate phone calls have been completed, the escort hour begins. Based on my listening experience, I would estimate that 95 percent of the calls involve some form of sex, although there are sessions when an escort will lounge around naked and never participate in any sexual activity.

Depending on the escort, she may have a number of complaints concerning the call. I reluctantly listen to the ladies I have termed the "bitchers and moaners." These ladies of the evening are constantly complaining about things like: the condo was disgusting, he hasn't showered in a week, a three-hundred-pound guy tried to get on top of her, he was condescending and verbally abusive, the john was too rough, and the list goes on. These objections are minor compared to the girls who actually are physically abused. In most cases, the escort brings trouble upon herself, especially if she is caught stealing, has a bad attitude, or is not offering full service without a tip. Recently, an escort didn't want to have sex with a Caribbean client for $150. When she wanted to leave, he called the cops. Apparently, the john was unaware that paying for sex is illegal in forty-nine states. Since she was there for an hour, the officer let the tramp go free with his money. Once the hooker has your money and she checks in, there are no refunds. If she leaves for any reason prior to your satisfaction, you're anything but screwed. The strumpet may tell you she has to give the money to her driver or they are going to send another girl, she may even offer you a free coupon for next time. Forget it, fool, your money is gone. An experienced escort will usually work with the client and resolve the conflict. If a girl gets caught stealing in the client's house, she runs the risk of getting injured in the house. While performing the cash 'n' dash, she may incur the client's wrath while outside the premises. One escort actually wears jean shorts under her dress should it be necessary to leave a hostile client. I have heard numerous accounts from the escorts who have had to run out naked with clothes in hand. It is also important for the escorts to know their way around a house should it be necessary to leave hastily. Almost all the girls carry mace, some have zappers, and one even had a gun.

One night, a hooker actually beat a wife up with her shoe when the unfortunate woman walked in on her husband while in the act of having sex with the escort. If an escort needs to leave the premises rapidly, she will call or text me. The car will be running and the passenger door opened for a quick getaway. This actually took place in the early morning hours in Hialeah. As the sun was rising, a Cuban escort was literally being chased out of the house by the mother of a young client. As the hooker was running into the car you could hear the mother screaming, "Puta, puta!" Quite the contrary took place in Hollywood. When a young Cuban client didn't have enough money, his mother actually handed the Brazilian escort the difference so her son could get laid.

SIX

Escort Confessions

Being there are a number of books written by escorts and their numerous experiences with their clients, I have chosen to publish only a handful of confessions. There are times when an escort will disclose the nature of a call, though not being a voyeur, I never ask unless they are visibly upset when returning to my car. All of the disclosures in this chapter are based on the experiences of escorts I have driven.

There are times the escorts participate in fetishes. One exceptionally unusual fetish was with a Japanese man who filled the hotel room with balloons and masturbated while the naked escort popped the balloons by sitting on them. A client once asked an escort to put on his dirty work shoes, and after half an hour she removed them so he could lick her nasty tasting feet. The escort may unexpectedly be asked to be a dominatrix, whereby the client expects her to tie him up with ropes, gag him, and then whip him, among other sexual acts. There are some clients who even enjoy the so-called "sweet milk" of lactating escorts.

Role-playing is sometimes required play. The client may

ask the bawd to wear certain lingerie or act as a schoolgirl by putting on a plaid skirt. Clients may dress up as a woman and want the escort to perform anal sex using a strap-on. There are even those special moments when the escort provides him with a golden shower, a hot plate, or places her finger with a condom in his ass. A common practice for the client's amusement is to offer the hooker a new dildo in an unopened package. Possession is nine-tenths of the law, so the dildo is hers to keep when she leaves the premises.

During any call there can be unexpected surprises. One unpolished escort experienced an agitated john when she ignored his command not to touch his arm. She didn't realize he suffered from premature ejaculation and a simple touch from her naked body would make him explode. Recently a new, young Russian escort went to a regular client. After the hour was up, she got in my car and kept repeating, "He is a sick man!" The escort denied it was anything to do with bestiality or anal perversion. It was so despicable she never talked about it and demanded to be driven straight home. Without question, I have never had a girl come out of a call so anguished.

One escort, on an extended call with a belligerent client, locked herself in the bathroom, left the water running, contacted me, and climbed out the window on the ground floor. Another situation arose when I had two girls in a call with three guys. The soon-to-be-groom was drunk, inconsolable, and getting angrier by the minute. I told the ladies to locate a sliding glass door and head for freedom.

Another escort went to a very exclusive mansion on a

couple's call. What she didn't realize at first was that the older man and the younger married woman were actually father and daughter. The incestuous relationship was revealed when she went to the bathroom and noticed family pictures on the wall.

There was an escort who was the last person to see the client alive. The escort went to the client's house, where he received a call that made him visibly distressed. According to the police, he was murdered immediately after she left the house. The homicide detective traced the last calls on his cell phone, and one of them was an agency number. The agency was contacted and the officer was instructed to contact the escort. Although she was apprehensive, she cooperated with the police, who were not interested in her occupation, but rather if she recalled the client receiving a call while in her presence.

I have a friend who is a former escort and had undoubtedly the most horrific experience when servicing a regular client in Boynton Beach, Florida. While practicing her profession, she apparently enraged this psychotic individual, who attempted to strangle her. The only reason she managed to escape was her regurgitating all over his white carpet. When he released his grip on her throat, she ran naked out the front door to her car. After she contacted police, he left town, only to murder more women as he journeyed across the U.S. This serial killer and local race car driver was on the FBI's most wanted list until he was eventually killed by police in a shootout in Maine.

SEVEN

Memorable Moments

Life as an escort driver is very similar to being a police officer on road patrol. We anticipate an uneventful, safe night, but we relish the adrenaline rush when suddenly exhilarating situations occur. I have listed a few of my most memorable moments.

As a driver, you must always be alert and quick thinking. During one early morning shift, while driving two strumpets, we decided to stop at a convenience store in Hallandale Beach. One of the hookers went into the ladies bathroom to smoke crack, and for the next thirty minutes got stuck in the mirror. As the line outside the lavatory backed up, the ladies in waiting petitioned an employee to do something. A nasty old lady started banging on the door. When the tramp opened the door, a heated verbal exchange took place. From my vantage point outside, I could see the employee go behind the counter and dial the police. Without hesitation, I ran into the store and told the two escorts to quickly get into my car; as we drove off, I immediately made a right turn and then a quick u-turn and headed for I-95. As we were getting on the entrance ramp heading north, we could see and hear two police cars coming from the opposite direction. We got off at the next exit, made two quick turns and then reversed direction and headed south on I-95. The goal was to drive five minutes, leave Broward County, and get off the highway in Dade County. All of us were relieved when we pulled into the dark, secluded office parking lot without any police presence. I mentioned to the dispatcher, "As hot as she is, her blatant attitude regarding her drug use will one day take the whole car down."

One slow night, I was sitting at a twenty-four-hour restaurant with two escorts when we were approached by a gentleman who was picking up dinner for his wife and employees of his local brothel. He was very proud of his new establishment and invited us to pay a visit. After careful deliberation and boredom, we decide to take a tour. The escorts were confused; they didn't realize this was no ordinary whorehouse, but a sham. The ladies working in this storefront were not expected to have sex any more than a stripper in a VIP room. Should a client complain, he would lose his money and be escorted from the premises by a huge bouncer. (The poor sap would still be horny, possibly broke, and couldn't call the police for a refund). The story doesn't end there. When we returned to the restaurant parking lot, the owner was waiting in his truck and paid one of the escorts $150 bucks for a blow job.

As an escort driver, I am sometimes called into service to perform duties above and beyond my job description. A Brazilian dispatcher once directed me to a specific hotel and provided me with a room number. When I reached my destination, I was expected to retrieve a valuable watch that had been lifted by an escort the previous night. The door of the hotel room opened, and I was confronted by her pimp. When he observed how forthright I was ("Where the hell is that thieving bitch?"), he was happy to disassociate himself and divulge her whereabouts. As I entered the hotel restaurant, I noticed a young blond who was just leaving. After introducing myself, I stated my goal to the crack head, expecting her to hand over the timepiece. Her contempt at the suggestion of returning the stolen item angered me. "If you don't give it to me now, the next person who confronts you may take a knife and slash your pretty face," I said. "Every time you look in the mirror and see that hideous scar, you will have wished you gave me the watch tonight." She paused for a moment, reached into her bra, cursed me, and then handed me the gold watch.

On a Wednesday evening, I took two escorts to a bachelor party in Fort Lauderdale. It started out as a one-hour, three-girl call. One of the escorts ended up staying in the mansion for sixteen hours, collecting $200 every hour. On two occasions, I went to the client's bank to cash his personal checks. I ended up breaking my own personal record, doing twenty-four calls in one night. Remarkably, it wasn't my most lucrative night. That happened when one of my regular escorts went on a private call for eleven hours at the end of our shift. I ended up with $900 for the evening/afternoon.

Another time, I was driving in South Beach when the escort requested I stop at a local convenience store. She noticed a car in the parking lot with three girls and a male driver. She recognized him as working for another service. I approached the car, told them I was a police officer, and demanded to see their identification. I accused them of being escorts and added that they were in serious trouble. One of the escorts was defiant and was insulted. The driver never once looked up, but after five minutes of acting authoritative, I told them I also worked for a service. Two hours later, my dispatcher called me, laughing hysterically and asking if he should thank me for making his night.

One evening in Hollywood, a hooker left the client's house completely drenched in sweat. As she got in my car, she told me to "max out the AC." When I hesitated to ask about her present state, she disclosed that the john didn't pay the electric or the water bill. However, he did have a small lamp that had been plugged into an extension cord running from his neighbor's house. I asked the sweaty hooker if she had received a tip for her discomfort. Remarkably, the gentleman was generous. (He clearly had his priorities in order.)

One of the escort services had an office that was located through the back door of a strip mall in Pompano Beach. I had to park and then use a code to enter the building. If I had a lucrative night, I would keep the drop money in a zippered bank bag in the trunk of my black convertible Camaro. One night as I proceeded to retrieve the money from the trunk, I was approached by two undercover narcotics agents. The hooker and I had unwittingly entered a stakeout. I told the officers I was here to say hello to a friend, never disclosing our real intention. They asked me to call him, and tell him I was outside. My calling him in an awkward manner allowed him the opportunity to cancel his shipment. Unbelievably, the vice squad had just subverted its own undercover operation. As it turns out, the dispatcher was expecting a different type of drop. It was his last night working for the agency. (It was a costly move for everyone. He was a competent dispatcher, but unfortunately his three-week replacement was horrendous).

On a hot, summer night I experienced my first direct encounter with police who were convinced I was driving two prostitutes. The first call of the night was located in Riviera Beach in Palm Beach County. As one of the ladies was checking in, a passing police cruiser observed the other escort smoking a cigarette in the condo parking lot. After the escort finished her cigarette, we proceeded to a local gas station. Forty minutes later, the escort checked out of the call. As we were returning to the condominium, I noticed there were three police cars on the same block with none of their lights on. Once the escort entered my car, I sternly stated to both ladies, "We are going to be pulled over, so listen carefully. Our story is that we are going to a swingers club in Fort Lauderdale and we met on a swinger's website." As anticipated, I was pulled over because the light above my license plate was not working. (Even if the light was working, police can always pull you over with the explanation: "A car matching your description was involved in a crime in the area.") When one of the officers asked where we were going, the story could not have played out better. None of the officers were familiar with the swinging lifestyle. They asked me to step out of the car and wanted to know if the girls were escorts. The officers asked if the ladies had asked me for money and if I had met them on a known hooker's website. Of course, I said no and mentioned the website for swinger hook-ups. A sagacious officer asked why I had left and then returned to the same location. I was quick to respond, "The lady wasn't ready when we got here, so we went to get gas to save time." With my deceptively sincere answers and a humorous swinger barbecue story, we were free to go. Fortunately for the escorts, who were both on probation and carrying illegal blues and bars, they weren't searched or checked for ID. The remainder of the evening was quite profitable as we did another six calls.

The evening/morning I will never forget started out no different than any other night. It was Friday night, and I picked up one of my regular girls around 10:40 P.M. I had occasionally driven her in the past when her primary driver was unavailable. It was a slow night, and we finally received a call in Hialeah around 12:30 A.M., which lasted for two hours. We decided to call it a night around 5 A.M., made the drop at the office, and headed north. We arrived at her apartment complex around 6 A.M., where I dropped her off in the parking area and headed home for some much-needed sleep. Less than a minute later, my cell phone rang. My first guess was that the escort had left something behind in the car. Upon answering the phone, I could only hear high-pitched wail (death scream). I tried to calm her down, and then I realized she was saying, "They're both dead."

When I arrived at her front door, it was ajar and I could see her roommate and his friend were both dead from gunshot wounds. This was my first crime scene where I was actually standing over two dead corpses. It was a surreal experience, knowing that their souls had recently departed from their lifeless bodies. The perpetrator was a cold-blooded killer who took the lives of two fathers. I knew I had to call the police while the escort tried to control her emotions. The police arrived in less than five minutes and quickly separated us while demanding our cell phones and identification. Prior to their arrival, I explained to her the importance of being truthful regarding our profession and the escort company that employed us. She was reluctant, having just finished probation for a DUI charge. When the detectives arrived around 8 A.M., I was placed in one of their cars and they recorded my account of the previous night's events. Initially, I saw myself as her alibi, but I quickly realized I was a person of interest and she was a prime suspect. It appeared to the police that the escort was the last person to see her roommate alive and the first one to find him dead. I, in turn, was in the area on both occasions.

As it turned out, the other gentleman who was murdered arrived at the apartment after I picked the escort up. I willingly submitted to a car search for the possible murder weapon. We both allowed them to take DNA samples because we had entered the crime scene. To leave no doubt of our innocence, we agreed to take a GSR (gunshot residue) examination to determine if either of us pulled the trigger or were in the room when the gun was discharged. To confirm our location throughout the evening, the police used UFED (universal forensic extraction device) technology on our phones to determine which cell towers were used when we made our calls. We complied with all the necessary procedures and were released seven hours later at 1 P.M. My children and I were surprised to find it was the lead story on the 11 P.M. nightly news. Two days later, the escort was driven to police headquarters, where she passed a lie detector test. As the case still remains unsolved, I am not at liberty to give any details that were not originally released to the media. Ironically, every escort knows that when she goes on a call she may find herself in a threatening situation. In this case, staying home would have been a deadly alternative.

EIGHT

My Sexual Exploits

I never intended to write this chapter, but after passing out my manuscript to a select few, I ascertained one simple truth: readers would rather be entertained than informed. For over twelve years, I delighted in sharing my stimulating swinger stories with friends and acquaintances. In comparison, my book seemed insipid. A woman reader had an excellent recommendation: try to recall one story from each of the more than one hundred ladies I have driven.

I am often asked if I receive any sexual perks from the escorts. (Isn't that the number one reason for becoming a driver?) Of the hundred or more ladies I have driven, there have been a select few I have had the desire to have sex with. Even so, a few of these ladies were strictly for oral gratification. There are very few escorts I want to see naked, so fellatio is the preferable alternative. Although there is usually a "driver discount," I can honestly say I have only paid twenty dollars three times for a hummer. These three ladies were going home with nothing in their pockets, so out of the kindness of my heart and with a firm boner, I indulged.

If any driver is going to have penetrating sex, I highly recommend you engage in the act at the beginning of the evening when the lady looks her hottest and smells her freshest. After five calls and ten hours on the job, there is a high probability of the driver being rejected.

As for my driving confessions, only once was I actually summoned by an escort to go into a call and help fulfill a woman's sexual fantasy. It was an afternoon couple's call at a hotel in Hialeah. The sexy Hispanic woman had never experienced DP (double penetration), so without hesitation or the promise of money I was overjoyed to fulfill her fantasy. (Customer satisfaction is clearly an important aspect of my profession.) Recently, I spoke to a woman client who called the service and was inquiring if I would be interested in performing a consensual rape scenario. She gave a brief description of her physical attributes and I was totally turned off, regardless of the pay she offered. As a discriminating gentleman, I would make a dreadful escort. (Maybe once a year, a woman will call a service looking for a male escort.)

Of all the escorts I have had sex with, one exceptional titillating twenty-three-year-old comes to mind. She had been my houseguest on numerous occasions, but her first visit was most notable. After returning to my dwelling from a hard night's work, she decided to enjoy a bowl of cereal. As I lifted her skirt and slipped it in doggy style, she acted like a skilled professional: never missing a spoonful, even when she heard my cry of ecstasy. (Her tramp stamp tattoo said it all: "Daddy's Little Girl.") It wasn't the first time I viewed her callipygian curves (firm round ass). At a client's mansion in Boca Raton, while in his driveway, I banged her from behind while speaking with the dispatcher. The other two jezebels were conveniently relaxing in the john's Jacuzzi.

There was one night in Jupiter when I was driving two hot ladies. One of them continued to extend on a party call, thus allowing me the opportunity to spend time with Miss Big Titty (I am guessing natural Fs). This attractive blond offered her finest oral service (topless, of course) if I successfully downloaded her desired ring tone on her phone. As I recollect, my stick of intense pleasure became instantaneously hard the moment her favorite song resounded.

The most common place for drivers and escorts to have sex is in the car. While driving through Sunny Isles one early morning, the escort and I spotted an attractive woman with her thumb in the air. I asked the hooker if she wouldn't mind if we offered her a ride. As she got in the car, we received a hotel call in Hollywood, Florida. After dropping the harlot at the front lobby, I explained to the hitchhiker the process of waiting until the escort checks in before we could leave the hotel parking area. After flirting for a few minutes and comparing tattoos, we decided it would be fair compensation if she gave me a blow job for driving her home. When the escort checked out of the hotel call early, she was surprised to see the woman still in the car. My explanation was simple: I was going to leave, but I had a feeling she might make this a fast call and I may not have been back in time. With a big smile on my face (the hitchhiker was talented), the three of us proceeded to the hitchhiker's destination before calling it a night.

One cold night while sitting in Fort Lauderdale, I made the decision to get a motel room with a prostitute. She was a very sensual woman in her thirties who enjoyed smoking crack. After she took a couple of hits on her crack pipe, we immediately undressed. As she leapt onto the bed, she said a phrase I will never forget: "How do you want me?" No doubt, this is a common hooker phrase.

My favorite place to have sex is the in-call. While employed for one conventional agency, I took it upon myself to make sure there were always clean towels and sheets. Working for the agency were two very cute, green-eyed twin spinners. Their popularity was known throughout the escort community, and clients offered large sums of money to book them simultaneously. Unfortunately for everyone involved, they were not bisexual and it was a total turn-off for them both. One evening, I was sent to the in-call to pick up one of the twins. She had just gotten out of the shower and asked me if I wanted to be her sex buddy. We immediately hit the sheets and spent the next two months having fun whenever possible. The next night I had to drive the other twin to a call. When she finished with the client, she asked me to drive her back to the in-call. She said, "I know you were with my sister last night. Now it's my turn." I have to admit they were different in bed, but equally satisfying.

Over the years, I have accompanied at least six escorts to my favorite swinger club in Fort Lauderdale. The first escort to join me was a Brazilian bombshell who boasted a sumptuous set of natural double-D breasts. Since I had been her private driver for the past few months, we had become sincere friends and never engaged in any sexual activity. After doing an afternoon call in Palm Beach County, we decided to stop by my house and view her new website. When my wife (now ex-wife) came home, the astonished look on her face was priceless. After realizing the nature of our business (we weren't having an afternoon fling in her bed), my reluctant spouse introduced herself and my children.

One slow evening, we made a spontaneous decision to call off and go to the swinger's club. The escort was feeling melancholy as she had just broken up with her boyfriend and needed a night on the town. Strippers, escorts, and nudists are a natural for the swinger lifestyle. Within fifteen minutes of entering the private club, we were approached by a sexy out-of-town couple. The chemistry was ideal, and we headed to the co-ed lockers. No sooner than our clothes were off, she hopped in the shower with the gentleman, while I proceeded to show the newly enhanced (breast enlargement) woman to the orgy beds. They eventually joined us, as did another couple, and we had a stimulating time. Although the Brazilian asked me to have sex with her, I politely refused. I was actually turned off after watching her have sex with at least six guys. The next day, she thanked me for an unforgettable night. It was obvious: the lady was perfect for the lifestyle.

A few years ago, I had the pleasure of taking an escort wearing a sexy leopard bra and panties to a Halloween Party at a swinger's club. When we got to the club, she remarked "I'm your bitch—whoever you want me to swap with, just let me know." During the night, we enjoyed the company of five couples. No doubt it could have been more, but I am a discerning gentleman. Unexpectedly, there was a reporter at the club that evening researching an article on the swinger sex clubs of South Florida. As fate would have it, the reporter was in the locker room when a man with blood dripping down his face and a frenzied woman entered. The reporter was quickly apprised of the situation. My date had unwittingly sat on the guy's schlong with no protection. When his girlfriend noticed, she went ballistic and punched her boyfriend in the nose. As blood dripped down his face, he followed his date out of the back room. I tried to console him by stating, "Even though your night is ruined, she is disease free." I had no clue if it was true or not, but it sounded reassuring.

There was another smoking-hot military couple who was also enjoying their company when this fiasco took place. When I informed the newbies as to what had just transpired, they weren't concerned. They responded by asking us to have sex with them as long as we used protection. We quickly replied with a resounding yes and enjoyed their company for the next two hours.

NINE

Is it Legal?

Whether having an escort service is legal or not is a very common question, but it has a circuitous answer. An escort service can legally operate in the three counties previously mentioned, usually under the adult entertainment category. If you read the first paragraph of a typical independent contractor agreement, like the one below, you will see quite clearly that there is no use of the word "sex" at any time. In Article 5, Part C and D, it specifically instructs all escorts to refrain from any behavior that may violate the Florida laws dealing with prostitution. However, if any escort abides by this contract, she will never work a second night for any service.

INDEPENDENT CONTRACTOR AGREEMENT

This contract is made between Escorts Inc., a Florida corporation (herein referred to as Escorts Inc.) and the undersigned Independent Contractor (herein referred to as Contractor). Escorts Inc. is in the business of referring entertainers for legitimate adult entertainment (specifically nude modeling and dancing) and for the purpose of companionship, and whereas

---

Escorts Inc. has offered to book the contractor to work as an entertainer and represents that they are 18 years old or more. It is agreed by parties as follows:

1. Contractor shall act as an entertainer with customers referred by and both parties acknowledge that she has the right to exercise control over how she deals with customers within the boundaries of decency and in accordance to the law.

2. Escorts Inc. shall pay the Contractor no salary. However, when quoting prices to prospective customers, the price shall include referral fee and a basic gratuity for the Contractor.

3. Escorts Inc. shall have no obligation for and not withhold any federal income taxes, Social Security, or any other taxes for which Contractor may be liable. Contractor understands that she will not be covered by unemployment compensation.

4. The Contractor shall be responsible for the payment of all state and federal taxes. The contractor specifically acknowledges that all estimated federal taxes, self-employment taxes, and Social Security taxes are her sole responsibility. Contractor will hold Escorts Inc. harmless from any tax liability.

5. Contractor Shall:

A. Work as an entertainer for those shifts agreed to each week. She shall arrive at her assignments promptly and not leave until her assignment is concluded.

B. Refrain from consuming unlawful drugs as an entertainer. She may drink alcohol in moderation if she is 21 years of age or older and if the alcohol is offered by her customer.

C. Obey all laws of the State of Florida, including the county and city in which she may be working. In particular,

Contractor shall refrain from any behavior which is lewd and lascivious or which violates the Florida laws dealing with prostitution.

D. An entertainer shall refrain from offering, soliciting, or accepting any unlawful propositions with respect to any customer, specifically those propositions which are in violation of the state laws regarding prostitution. She shall also refrain from any sexual contact in violation of any state or local law and any unlawful touching of a customer's genitals. ANY VIOLATION OF THIS RULE WILL RESULT IN IMMEDIATE TERMINATION OF THIS AGREEMENT.

E. All entertainers shall refrain from giving the customer her phone number, address, or intentionally meeting with the customer outside of her immediate assignment. ANY VIOLATION OF THIS RULE WILL RESULT IN THE IMMEDIATE TERMINATION OF THIS AGREEMENT.

F. The entertainer shall collect all fees from the customer and deliver all fees at the end of her shift.

6. The parties understand and agree that should Contractor leave prior to the end of her assignment or fail to appear for an assignment or fail to work any shift for which she has agreed to work, without an acceptable, documented reason, she will be subject to dismissal and/or fines.

7. Either party may terminate this agreement with or without reason at any time.

DATE:_____

NAME OF CONTRACTOR:_____

SIGNATURE OF CONTRACTOR:_____

One of the agencies I worked for during the writing of this book had been in operation for over ten years. The agency had the impudence to advertise on a digital billboard on I-95 in Fort Lauderdale, with favorable results. This bold initiative is rare in an industry that normally prefers to fly under the radar. I had a chance to speak with the owner on a slow night, and we discussed why other agencies have not shared the same success. Our verbal exchange was prompted by the previous evening's news that an escort agency had been shut down and four people were arrested. The TV reporter said there had been a three-year undercover investigation regarding prostitution. There are at least three reasons any agency may be targeted by the authorities:

1. Underage girls

2. Selling drugs from the office or using the ladies to distribute

3. Failure to pay taxes

The Palm Beach County Sheriff's Department has a specific unit that mainly focuses on arresting street-walkers. The reluctance of escorts to discuss their sexual intentions prior to collecting the money is a difficult obstacle for officers to overcome when trying to conduct a sting operation. Surprisingly, the departed DC Madam, when being interviewed by ABC News *20/20*, admitted that her service was designed to fulfill sexual fantasies. When dealing with a dubious john, I recommend the escorts use the phrase "I am here for time and companionship." I have known tentative call girls who insisted that a client expose himself before discussing anything of a sexual nature. If a client is suspicious and insisting a hooker reveal her carnal intentions, then she should sit next to him and stroke his upper thigh. If he is a vice cop, he will become restless. If he is a paying customer, he will encourage the escort to grasp the one-eyed serpent. When in doubt, if he ain't whipping it out, it's time to get out. Broward and Dade County have a task force that continually does hotel and even condominium stings. They use known prostitution websites, which feature independent escorts as well as calling local escort agencies.

Last month, an escort went on a call to a luxurious hotel in Miami and, along with ten other hookers, was arrested for solicitation of prostitution. The shirtless undercover officer pretended to be drunk while the hookers incriminated themselves. Two of the prostitutes were also arrested for robbery when the vice cop went to the bathroom and they attempted to pilfer his wallet and jewelry, which was atop the dresser. Unfortunately for these escorts, they were arrested in Dade County, which is notorious for having the most repugnant incarceration facilities in the tricounty area. The driver was also arrested when he went into rescue mode and knocked on the hotel door. When the hour was up and the escort did not answer her phone, the driver should have anonymously called hotel security and casually waited near the john's room. He would have quickly realized there was a police presence and quietly retreated to the elevator.

On rare occasions, the task force will use the same independent site and do a reverse sting using undercover policewomen posing as prostitutes. It is preposterous if the authorities believe they can reduce the number of escorts with their minimal amount of arrests. I surmise their efforts are focused on ladies possessing drugs, having outstanding warrants, underage girls, illegal aliens, and sex trafficking.

Since it is established that escort agencies are legal throughout South Florida, then how is it that a driver working for a legitimate business can be arrested for transportation of prostitution? This actually happened to two drivers in Miami, who dropped off the individual escorts on a two-girl call. Ironically, both hookers had fruit names, and trust me, they were rotten fruit. Unlike my first escort-driving position, where I collected the money and/or negotiated a fee, these two drivers had no contact with the police until they were approached and arrested in the hotel parking lot. Escort drivers are occasionally harassed by local police, but these two ill-fated gentlemen spent the weekend in jail.

There is a federal law known as the Mann Act, which was passed on June 25, 1910. It is named after Congressman James Robert Mann and in its original form prohibited white slavery and the interstate transport of females for immoral purposes. It was later amended by Congress in 1978, and again in 1986, to apply only to transport for the purpose of prostitution or illegal sexual acts. Whoever knowingly transports any individual in interstate or foreign commerce, or in any territory or possession of the United States, with intent that such individual will engage in prostitution, or in any sexual activity for which any person can be charged with a criminal offense, or attempts to do so, shall be fined under this title or imprisoned not more than ten years, or both. In 1960, the notorious Charles Manson was actually convicted of violating the Mann Act by taking two prostitutes from California to New Mexico to work.

Closing Comments

Although I do not judge any prostitute for the choice she has made, as a loving father of a teenage daughter, I am strongly opposed to any woman becoming an escort.

There is no question in my mind that the world's oldest profession will always exist. So for those gentleman and select ladies who dare to indulge, here are a few pearls of wisdom:

1. Always have proper respect for the lady-in-red you have requested.

2. Always have at least $50–$100 more than the negotiated price; it is worth the extra money. Hold on to your extra cash, especially if they try using the hooker baby hustle (e.g., they need money to buy milk and diapers for a fictitious infant at home.)

3. Always use protection, even if not required.

4. Always hooker-proof your house. Conceal all money, jewelry, cologne, and any possession of value prior to an escort arriving. They just can't resist taking a souvenir.

5. Under any circumstances, do not allow the call girl to leave the premises after you hand her the cash. She can pay her driver after you have been serviced.

6. Always read the reviews posted on a website known as the IndiBoard before calling your local agency.

The bottom line is, if you are fortunate enough to find a company that consistently provides you with women who are desirable, pleasing, and honest, then stay loyal, my friend.

Now that you have read *She's At Your Door,* you know more about the escort profession than you probably cared to. With the completion off this book, I will no longer be in the driver's seat. I am currently working on my next book, regarding my erotic personal swinger stories.

About the Author

Vince Golia was born and raised on the perilous streets of the Bronx, New York. After having been stabbed and narrowly missing being taken out by a bullet, he had a spiritual awakening and decided to study theology. In 1983 he graduated from Iona College in New Rochelle, New York, and taught theology at the Academy of the Resurrection in Rye, New York.

When he married in 1990, he desired a peaceful life for his future family and moved to South Florida with his wife. In 1992, he was hired at Cardinal Gibbons High School in Ft. Lauderdale, where he taught religious studies for three years. He was forced to retire from teaching when he was blacklisted for reporting the unwanted sexual advances of the now-retired principal who was a Piarist priest.

Vince was one of the first Saturn car salesmen in the nation and has held numerous sales positions over the past twenty years. He also spent two years working with a number of talent agencies acting in television commercials. Realizing the important role computers would play in our daily lives, Vince received his MCSE (Microsoft Certified Systems Engineer) certification from PC Professor in 2001.

His main interests include weightlifting, racquetball and the martial arts. By avocation, Vince has devoted countless hours to the study of entomology. He has traveled to a number of countries and maintains a renowned, diverse personal insect collection. He has discovered over a dozen new insect species and has three species (two beetles, *Ischyrus goliai* and *Scirtes goliai,* and a plant hopper, *Toya goliai*) named after him. Vince has also coauthored two papers pertaining to exotic Asian insects that he first discovered in Florida. He has recently discovered a new ladybug in South Florida and plans to name it after his daughter.

Vince has been blessed with two exceptionally astute children. His son is a student at the University of Florida and his daughter is in high school.

The author is available for questions and speaking engagements at goliav4@gmail.com.

www.ingramcontent.com/pod-product-compliance
Lightning Source LLC
Chambersburg PA
CBHW070851280326
41934CB00008B/1392